FELIX HARCOURT
MINISTRIES

Felix Harcourt Ministries
P.O. Box 134, Stacy, MN 55079
fhmi.net

Copyright © 2023 Felix Harcourt.

All rights reserved. No part of this book may be reporduced or used in any manner without the prior written permission of the copyright owner, except for the use of brief quotations in a book review.

Paperback: 978-1-0880-8878-4

All scripture referenced is from the International Children's Bible (ICB).

God's Word Gives Life

Healing Devotional

Felix Harcourt

Author's Prayer

Father, Lord, in the Name of Jesus Christ. I pray for every child reading this book now that you will manifest your glory in their lives through the pages of this book. I pray that the scriptures will come alive and restore their health as they read, memorize, and meditate in Jesus' Name. I pray their faith strengthens and reflects their confession. Thank you, Lord, for answered prayer in Jesus' Name. Amen.

Acknowledgement

Thanks to My wife, Nonye, for her encouragement. Mr & Mrs. Kas, who ran with the vision. Oni & Ume, my daughters who kindly gave their feedback, Nick & Sue Olivanti for editing, and all FHMI financial partners.

The Story Behind The Book

Few years ago, I separated myself for four weeks to spend time with the Lord in prayer and fasting. The experience in God's presence was wonderful and beyond description. The vision for this devotional was born from that experience. In a session of deep prayer and meditation, I saw myself in the children's ward of a hospital where I received instruction from the Lord to reach kids with a message of healing because they are innocent, as the strategy of the devil is to eliminate and destroy their future and destiny through sickness and disease.

It's not His [God's] will for the kids to be sick. Neither is He the one permitting sickness in their lives. Satan is the one behind their illness, just like the days of Moses when he went after the lives of kids through King Pharaoh. In the days of Jesus Christ, God's beloved Son, Satan the wicked one, went after kids through king Herod. That's how he's going after kids through different kinds of sickness and diseases.

It was an eye-opener to me, so it should be to every Christian that the devil is behind the attack on kids. The scripture said the thief comes to steal and kill and destroy. But I came to give life—life in all its fullness. John 10:10 (ICB).

The thief here is referred to as the devil. He is the wicked one. He is the one behind all evil. Jesus Christ came to give life, and He has given us that life through what He did on the cross. We got that life immediately as we gave our lives to Him. The scripture makes it clear in 1 John 5:11-12 (ICB). This is what God told us: God has given us eternal life, and this life is in his Son. Whoever has the Son has life. But the person who does not have the Son of God does not have life.

The life of the Father working in the Son, that same life is right inside of everyone who has accepted Jesus Christ as his personal Lord and savior. You know about Jesus from Nazareth. God made him the Christ by giving him the Holy Spirit and power. You know how Jesus went everywhere doing good. He healed those who were ruled by the devil, for God was with Jesus. Acts 10:38 (ICB).

He sent us to represent Him. He sent us to do the exact thing He was doing, and He will still do it through us when we yield to Him. When we do that, we become His extension. That's what He was telling me in the vision. He was telling me to become His extension which I willingly accepted, and the rest, He takes the glory.

This devotional provides scriptures and confession to saturate the mind with the word of God. It will cause faith to grow and bring health and healing as you read, meditate, and confess the word.

My child, pay attention to my words. Listen closely to what I say. Don't ever forget my words. Keep them deep within your heart. These words are the secret to life for those who find them. They bring health to the whole body. Proverbs 4:20 -22 (ICB).

This devotional is dedicated to all kids.

Day 1

If you declare with your mouth, "Jesus is Lord". and if you believe in your heart that God raised Jesus from death, then you will be saved. We believe with our hearts, and so we are made right with God. And we declare with our mouths to say that we believe, and so we are saved. Romans 10:9-10

Then you will joyfully give thanks to the Father. He has made you able to have all that he has prepared for his people who live in the light. Colossians 1:12

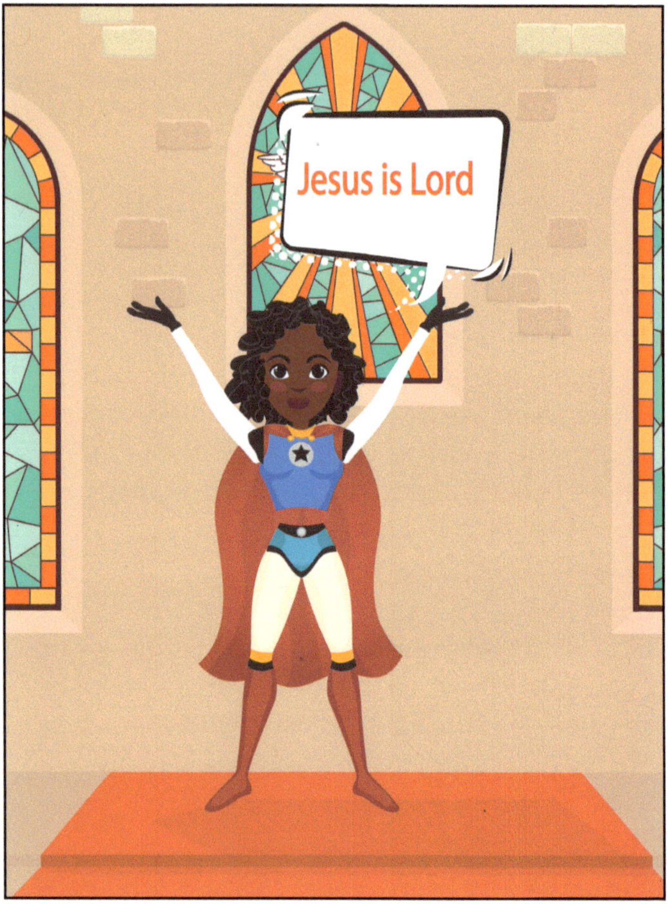
Jesus is Lord

Confession

I am the glory of God; I am His righteousness; I am His dwelling place, I am a partaker of His divine nature, and I have been created for the God kind of life!

Day 2

Dear friends, we should love each other, because love comes from God. The person who loves has become God's child and knows God. Whoever does not love does not know God, because God is love. 1 John 4:7-8

That evening people brought to Jesus many who had demons. Jesus spoke, and the demons left them. Jesus healed all the sick. Matthew 8:16

Confession

I refuse to be moved by how I feel in my body! My faith in Christ is the victory that overcomes every illness! Therefore, I confess that my faith is alive and producing results in me and for me! I agree and believe the Word of God and I am strong in faith. Glory to God!

Day 3

While the boy was coming, the demon threw him on the ground. The boy lost control of himself. But Jesus gave a strong command to the evil spirit. Then the boy was healed, and Jesus gave him back to his father. Luke 9:42

I do not live anymore—it is Christ living in me. I still live in my body, but I live by faith in the Son of God. He loved me and gave himself to save me. Galatians 2:20

Confession

Christ lives in me; therefore, no sickness or infection can stay in my body. Jesus carried my disease on His body so that I may never experience any illness in my body. I confess today that my body is strong and healthy! Sickness has no place in me; the life of Christ is at work in every cell, muscle, bone and organ in my body in Jesus' Name. Amen!

Day 4

Publius' father was very sick with a fever and dysentery. But Paul went to him and prayed. Then he put his hands on the man and healed him. Acts 28:8

For God loved the world so much that he gave his only Son. God gave his Son so that whoever believes in him may not be lost, but have eternal life. John 3:16

Confession

Christ is Lord over my spirit, soul, and body. Therefore, no illness or disease has any place in me. No weapon formed against me will prosper. Jesus has all authority over my body, and I confess that I dwell daily in health and strength in Jesus' Name. Amen.

Day 5

But they would not answer his question. So Jesus took the man, healed him, and sent him away. Luke 14:4

Yes, I am sure that nothing can separate us from the love God has for us. Not death, not life, not angels, not ruling spirits, nothing now, nothing in the future, no powers, nothing above us, nothing below us, or anything else in the whole world will ever be able to separate us from the love of God that is in Christ Jesus our Lord. Romans 8:39

Confession

I am born of God; my origin is in Him! No sickness has the power or ability to destroy my body. I have the overcoming life of God in me, that has given me the victory over sickness and disease.

Day 6

He did these things to make come true what Isaiah the prophet said: "He took our suffering on him. And he felt our pain for us." Matthew 8:17

But Christ died for us while we were still sinners. In this way, God shows his great love for us. Romans 5:8

Confession

The Holy Spirit lives in me; therefore, I have the power of God to effect changes. I refuse to permit anything contrary to God's Word in my body. As I speak out God's Word, I experience positive changes in my body in Jesus's Name Amen.

Day 7

Many of these people had evil spirits in them. But Philip made the evil spirits leave them. The spirits made a loud noise when they came out. There were also many weak and crippled people there. Philip healed them, too. Acts 8:7

But if someone obeys God's teaching, then God's love has truly arrived at its goal in him. This is how we know that we are following God. 1 John 2:5

Confession

I am the Temple of the Holy Spirit, and my body functions for God. Therefore, every cell and organ in my body complies with the Word of God. The power of the Holy Spirit sustains my body. I confess that the Holy Spirit is at work in me; therefore, my body is renewed daily. I live continually in health through the working power of the Holy Spirit in me.

Day 8

Jesus healed many who had different kinds of sicknesses. He also forced many demons to leave people. But he would not allow the demons to speak, because they knew who he was. Mark 1:34

God did not give us a spirit that makes us afraid. He gave us a spirit of power and love and self-control. 2 Timothy 1:7

Confession

As I receive the Word of God into my heart, I confess that it is working in me, producing the results it talks about in my body. The Word of God is life and health to my baby. Its transforming power is changing my life's circumstances and causing my health to spring forth in Jesus' Name Amen.

Day 9

A woman was there who had been bleeding for 12 years. She had spent all her money on doctors, but no doctor was able to heal her. Luke 8:43

When the woman saw that she could not hide, she came forward, shaking. She bowed down before Jesus. While all the people listened, she told why she had touched him. Then, she said, she was healed immediately. Luke 8:47

God has chosen you and made you his holy people. He loves you. So always do these things: Show mercy to others; be kind, humble, gentle, and patient. Colossians 3:12

Confession

Nothing is impossible to me. Therefore, I take responsibility for the direction of my life. My tongue is wholesome, and it is a tree of life; I speak the right words and channel my life in the right direction in the Name of Jesus. Amen.

Day 10

Christ carried our sins in his body on the cross. He did this so that we would stop living for sin and start living for what is right. And we are healed because of his wounds. 1 Peter 2:24

If you love only the people who love you, then you will get no reward. Even the tax collectors do that. Matthew 5:46

Confession

My faith is the victory that overcomes every challenge to my health. I believe God's Word that says the stripes of Jesus healed me. Therefore, my health shines forth today and every day in Jesus' Name. Amen.

Day 11

You know about Jesus from Nazareth. God made him the Christ by giving him the Holy Spirit and power. You know how Jesus went everywhere doing good. He healed those who were ruled by the devil, for God was with Jesus. Acts 10:38

You have heard that it was said, "Love your neighbor and hate your enemies." But I tell you, love your enemies. Pray for those who hurt you. Matthew 5:43-44

Confession

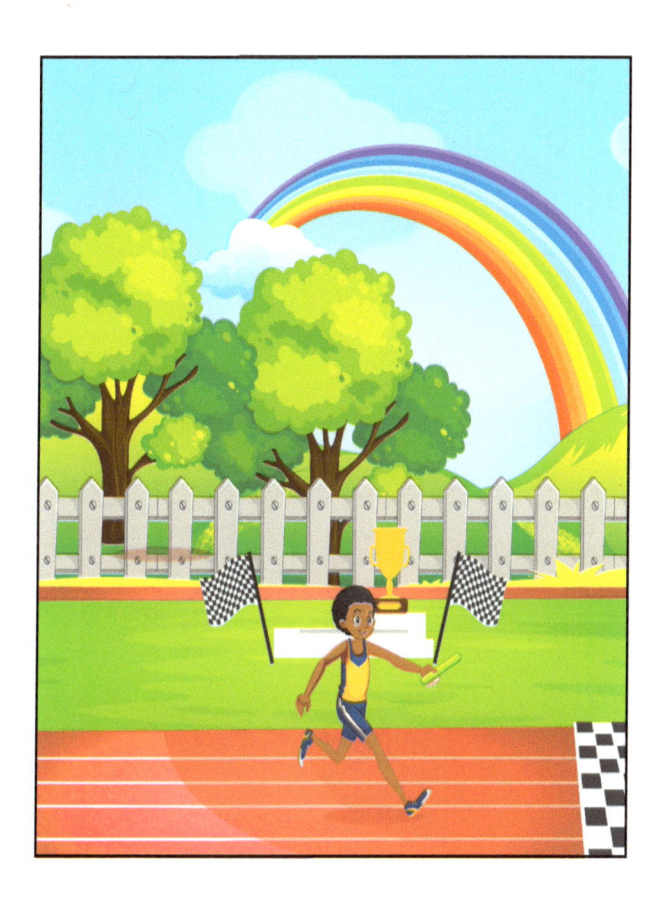

I hold on to God's Word, no matter what I see or hear. I am an overcomer, and I live the overcoming life. I do not fight the devil because he has been defeated already. Instead, I am conscious of my victory in Christ Jesus and I walk in the light of God's word, and I am free from every sickness. In Jesus' Name. Amen.

Day 12

After this, all the other sick people on the island came to Paul, and he healed them, too. Acts 28:9

But God's mercy is great, and he loved us very much. We were spiritually dead because of the things we did wrong against God. But God gave us new life with Christ. You have been saved by God's grace. Ephesians 2:4-5

Confession

I speak out my faith and confess that what God's Word says I have is mine now. As I discover what I have in Christ and say it, I will indeed have a praise report. I live in faith, and the beauty and glory of God shines through me. In Jesus' Name, Amen.

Day 13

Crowds came from all the towns around Jerusalem. They brought their sick and those who were bothered by evil spirits. All of them were healed. Acts 5:16

This is how God showed his love to us: He sent his only Son into the world to give us life through him. True love is God's love for us, not our love for God. God sent his Son to die in our place to take away our sins. That is how much God loved us, dear friends! So we also must love each other. 1 John 4:9-11

Confession

God's Word nourishes my spirit, refreshes my soul, and is healthy for my body. I pay attention to God's Word and believe what it says about me. God's Word says I am healed. I believe it with my heart and I confess it with my mouth. I am healed.

Day 14

When the sun went down, the people brought their sick to Jesus. They had many different diseases. Jesus put his hands on each sick person and healed every one of them. Luke 4:40

So be humble under God's powerful hand. Then he will lift you up when the right time comes. Give all your worries to him, because he cares for you. 1 Peter 5:6-7

Confession

I believe in the power of God's Word. My faith wins all the time; it is proof-producing and brings forth praise reports. My health springs forth quickly, and I reflect God's goodness.

Day 15

When one of them saw that he was healed, he went back to Jesus. He praised God in a loud voice. Luke 7:15

The Father has loved us so much! He loved us so much that we are called children of God. And we really are his children. But the people in the world do not understand that we are God's children, because they have not known him. 1 John 3:1

Confession

I have been given the power of attorney to use the name of Jesus. Therefore, I reject every sickness in my body. The work of Satan in my body is broken and destroyed in Jesus' Name. Amen.

Day 16

Jesus knew what the Pharisees were doing, so he left that place. Many people followed him, and he healed all who were sick. Matthew 12:15

I give you a new command: Love each other. You must love each other as I have loved you. All people will know that you are my followers if you love each other. John 13:34-35

Confession

I declare that Satan has no authority or place in my health and all that concerns me. The name of the Lord Jesus has all power and authority. Therefore, in His name, I prevail against sickness.

Day 17

But the news about Jesus was spreading more and more. Many people came to hear Jesus and to be healed of their sicknesses. Luke 5:15

And so we know the love that God has for us, and we trust that love. God is love. Whoever lives in love lives in God, and God lives in him. If God's love is made perfect in us, then we can be without fear on the day God judges us. We will be without fear, because in this world we are like him. 1 John 4:16-17

Confession

I am in Christ Jesus and totally immersed in Him. Everything about my life is reflecting God's glory. I walk bold and fearless, full of faith and confidence, divinely protected from all evil, and made victorious in Christ Jesus.

Day 18

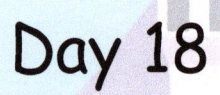

They all came to hear Jesus teach and to be healed of their sicknesses. He healed those who were troubled by evil spirits. Luke 6:18

Where God's love is, there is no fear, because God's perfect love takes away fear. It is punishment that makes a person fear. So love is not made perfect in the person who has fear. We love because God first loved us. 1 John 4:18-19

Confession

I have been given the authority and ability to drive out devils in the name of Jesus. I exercise that authority now and frustrate Satan's influence in my life in Jesus's Name Amen.

Day 19

All the people were trying to touch Jesus, because power was coming from him and healing them all! Luke 6:19

That is why I did not come to you myself. You only need to say the word, and my servant will be healed. Luke 7:7

I give you a new command: Love each other. You must love each other as I have loved you. John 13:34

Confession

I refuse to be afraid in this life; for I am strong in the grace that is in Christ Jesus. Fear has lost its power over me; for greater is He in me than he that is in the world. The Word of God has taken full possession of me through my spirit, soul, and body.

Day 20

Jesus said to the officer, "I will go and heal him." Matthew 8:7

Jesus called his 12 followers together. He gave them power to drive out evil spirits and to heal every kind of disease and sickness. Mathew 10:1

If someone says, "I love God," but hates his brother, he is a liar. He can see his brother, but he hates him. So he cannot love God, whom he has never seen. And God gave us this command: Whoever loves God must also love his brother. 1 John 4:20-21

Confession

Thank you, Lord, for the power of your Word in my life. I am built and nourished by your Word for a life of health. My mind is renewed, and the power of your Word transforms my life.

Day 21

Jesus was not able to work many miracles there. The only miracles he did were to heal some sick people by putting his hands on them. Mark 6:5

The followers forced many demons out and poured olive oil on many sick people and healed them. Mark 6:13

He who knows my commands and obeys them is the one who loves me. And my Father will love him who loves me. I will love him and will show myself to him. John 14:21

Confession

I am not of this world. I am born of God, and I live the life of God here on earth. I am conscious of my divine rights, and I enjoy supernatural health.

Day 22

When she touched his coat, her bleeding stopped. She could feel in her body that she was healed. Mark 5:29

There were also some women with him who had been healed of sicknesses and evil spirits. One of the women was Mary, called Magdalene, from whom seven demons had gone out. Luke 8:2

This is my command: Love each other as I have loved you. John 15:12

Confession

I refuse to be afraid in this life because I am strong in the grace that is in Christ Jesus. Fear has lost its power over me, for greater is He in me than he that is in the world. The Word of God has taken full possession of me through my spirit, soul, and body.

Day 23

Heal the sick. Give dead people life again. Heal those who have harmful skin diseases. Force demons to leave people. I give you these powers freely. So help other people freely. Matthew 10:8

In the synagogue, there was a man with a crippled hand. Some Jews there were looking for a reason to accuse Jesus of doing wrong. So they asked him, "Is it right to heal on the Sabbath day? Matthew 12:10

A thief comes to steal and kill and destroy. But I came to give life—life in all its fullness. John 10:10

Confession

The eyes of my understanding are enlightened to know my right in Christ. I take full control of my health, and I command Satan to stay away from my life in Jesus' Name Amen.

Day 24

They saw the crippled man standing there beside the two apostles. They saw that the man was healed. So they could say nothing against them. Acts 4:14

This man was listening to Paul speak. Paul looked straight at him and saw that the man believed God could heal him. Acts 14:9

But the Spirit gives love, joy, peace, patience, kindness, goodness, faithfulness, gentleness, self-control. There is no law that says these things are wrong. Galatians 5:22-23

Confession

The Word of God is my life and sustenance and has made me fruitful in every good work. I live in divine health, supernatural abundance, and in continual victory over sickness. The light of God's Word illuminates my path, and all things are working together for my good, in Jesus' Name. Amen.

Day 25

The Spirit of the Lord is in me. This is because God chose me to tell the Good News to the poor. God sent me to tell the prisoners of sin that they are free, and to tell the blind that they can see again. God sent me to free those who have been treated unfairly. Luke 4:18

When Jesus arrived, he saw a large crowd. He felt sorry for them and healed those who were sick. Matthew 14:14

My dear friend, I know your soul is doing well. I pray that you are doing fine in every way and that your health is good. 3 John 1:2

Confession

I have been given the power of attorney to use the name of Jesus. Therefore, I reject every sickness in my body. The work of Satan in my body is broken and destroyed in Jesus' Name. Amen.

The eyes of my understanding are enlightened to know my right in Christ. I take complete control of my health, and I command Satan to stay away from my life in Jesus' Name. Amen.

Day 26

The news about Jesus spread all over Syria, and people brought all the sick to him. These sick people were suffering from different kinds of diseases and pain. Some were suffering very great pain, some had demons, some were epileptics, and some were paralyzed. Jesus healed all of them. Matthew 4:24

Then Jesus said to the officer, "Go home. Your servant will be healed just as you believed he would." And at that same time his servant was healed. Matthew 8:13

In Christ we were chosen to be God's people. God had already chosen us to be his people, because that is what he wanted. And God is the One who makes everything agree with what he decides and wants. Ephesians 1:11

Confession

I declare that Satan has no authority or place in my health and all that concerns me. The name of the Lord Jesus has all power and authority. Therefore, in his name, I prevail against sickness.

Day 27

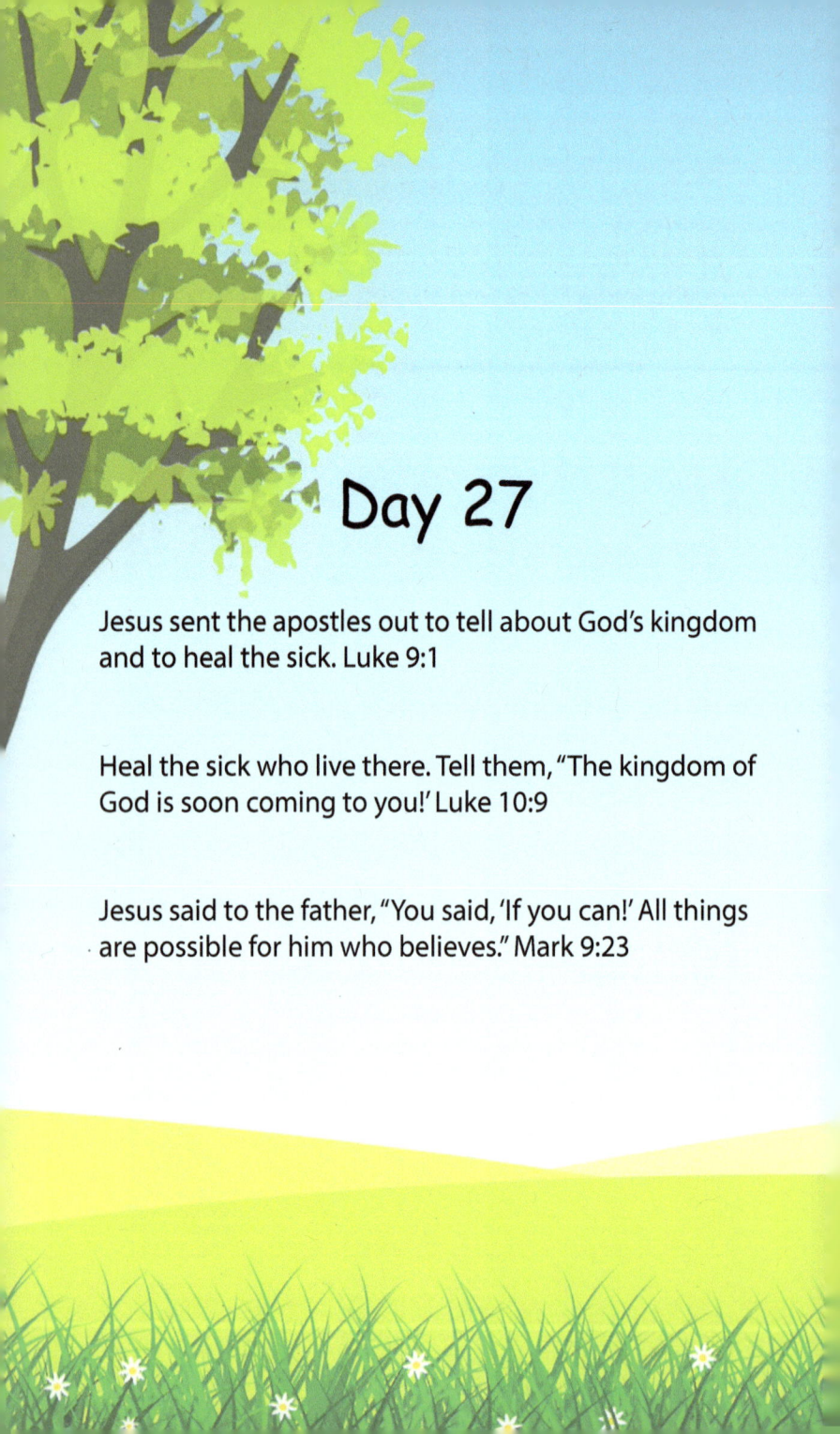

Jesus sent the apostles out to tell about God's kingdom and to heal the sick. Luke 9:1

Heal the sick who live there. Tell them, "The kingdom of God is soon coming to you!' Luke 10:9

Jesus said to the father, "You said, 'If you can!' All things are possible for him who believes." Mark 9:23

Confession

I am in Christ; Christ Jesus lives in me and I am totally immersed in Him. Everything about my life is reflecting God's glory. I walk bold and fearless, full of faith and confidence, divinely protected from all evil, and made victorious in Christ Jesus.

Day 28

Jesus said, "Stop!" Then he touched the servant's ear and healed him. Luke 22:51

But the man who had been healed did not know who it was. There were many people in that place, and Jesus had left. John 5:13

But now Christ has made you God's friends again. He did this by his death while he was in the body, that he might bring you into God's presence. He brings you before God as people who are holy, with no wrong in you, and with nothing that God can judge you guilty of. Colossians 1:22

Confession

I have been given the authority and ability to drive out devils in the name of Jesus. I exercise that authority now and frustrate the influence of Satan in my life in Jesus' Name Amen.

Day 29

But the people learned where Jesus went and followed him. Jesus welcomed them and talked with them about God's kingdom. He healed those who needed to be healed. Luke 9:11

Large crowds followed Jesus, and he healed them there. Matthew 19:2

Confess your sins to each other and pray for each other. Do this so that God can heal you. When a good man prays, great things happen. James 5:16

Confession

I hold on to God's Word, no matter what I see or hear. I am an overcomer, and I live the overcoming life. I do not fight the devil because he has been defeated already. Instead, I walk in the consciousness of my victory in Christ Jesus. Today I walk free of every sickness and Walk in the light of God's Word. In Jesus' Name. Amen.

Day 30

The blind and crippled people came to Jesus in the Temple, and Jesus healed them. Mattew 21:14

The men who saw these things happen told the others all about how Jesus had made the man well. Luke 8:36

Confession

Thank you, Lord, for the power of your Word in my life. I am built and nourished by your Word for a life of health. My mind is renewed, and the power of your Word transforms my life.

Day 31

Jesus said to the Pharisees and teachers of the law, "Is it right or wrong to heal on the Sabbath day?" Luke 14: 3

The man heard that Jesus had come from Judea and was now in Galilee. He went to Jesus and begged him to come to Capernaum and heal his son. His son was almost dead. John 4:47

Then God said, "Let us make human beings in our image and likeness. And let them rule over the fish in the sea and the birds in the sky. Let them rule over the tame animals, over all the earth and over all the small crawling animals on the earth." So God created human beings in his image. In the image of God he created them. He created them male and female. Genesis 1:26-27

Confession

I am not of this world. I am born of God and live the life of heaven here on earth. I am conscious of my heavenly rights, and I enjoy supernatural health.

Author's Note

Speaking God's Word Out Loud

Before God and Christ Jesus, I give you a command. Christ Jesus confessed that same great truth when he stood before Pontius Pilate. And God gives life to everything. Now I tell you: (1 Timothy 6:13). International Children's Bible (ICB)

Here, "Confession" is translated from the Greek word "Homologia," which means to speak the same thing in consent. So confessing the Word of God means you agree with the word and say what the Word of God says about you, Himself, your world, or anyone or situation.

Why is it so important that we confess the Word boldly? It's because our confessions create realities. Jesus said, "You shall have what you say" (Mark 11:23). What are the things you're supposed to say? They're the same things God has already declared in the Scriptures.

Hebrews 13:5-6 says, "…God has said…So we can feel sure and say…." The reason He said what He said is so that we may boldly say the same thing. God's Word isn't for you to hear and be quiet; you respond by saying the same thing. That's a true confession of the Word. God gave you the Word, so you'll boldly proclaim it.

Someone might ask, "Must I say it?" Emphatically yes! Otherwise, you'll never experience the vital reality of the Word of God in your life. It's the way to get your spirit to take hold of the Word to become a reality in your life. The Christian life is lived by words; it's for talkers, talkers of the Word. Perhaps you know someone who's been attacked by cancer, diabetes, or any sickness; advise them not to keep quiet! They should have "talking sessions." You say, "What if they're too weak to talk?" Let them mutter or even whisper: "I have the life of God in me; the Spirit that raised up Jesus from the dead lives in me; therefore, my whole body is quickened and energized with divine life. No sickness can stay in my body. The presence of God's Spirit destroys every trace of sickness and disease in my body."

If they mutter it long enough, it'll turn into a shout, and soon enough, they'll bounce off that sickbed. God's Word is medicine. It cures every sickness and keeps you in divine health.

God's Word is God

Before the world began, there was the Word. The Word was with God, and the Word was God. (John 1:1) International Children's Bible (ICB)
One of the extraordinary ways the Lord manifests Himself is in and through the Word. The Word of God created the universe. The Word of God is life. The Word of God is power. The Word of God is light. The Word of God is truth. The Word of God is God. Where the Word of God is, God is!

The Word of God isn't like the Word of a man. Centering your mind on the Word is centering your mind on God. The Bible says He keeps in perfect peace—peace of health—the one whose mind is stayed on Him (Isaiah 26:3). The way to stay your mind on Him is by meditating on the Word.

The Holy Spirit never does anything without the Word. For example, in Genesis chapter one, we read that God created the heavens and the earth in the beginning. But the earth was without form and was empty and covered with darkness. Then the Spirit of God moved over the face of the waters, but nothing changed. The earth was still a chaotic mass until God said, "Let there be light," and light became. The Spirit of God caused the light to manifest. He acted on the Word. Until the Word is given, the Spirit does nothing.

Don't ignore the Word; some Christians ignore the Word, and that's so unwise. What you need for the miracle you desire; what you need to prevail in any crisis and live every day in victory is the Word.

When you face challenges, when things get tough and rough, keep your confidence in the Word. Refuse to compromise. Get radical with your faith, affirmation and confession of the Word. As you speak, the Spirit will cause things to happen regarding your words because the Word of God in your mouth is God talking! It'll always prevail.

A Prayer of Salvation

Will you be willing to accept His Lordship and friendship?
If you do, then make this confession.

Say this: "O Lord God, I believe with all my heart in Jesus Christ, Son of the living God. I believe He died for me, and God raised Him from the dead. I believe He's alive today. Therefore, I confess with my mouth that Jesus Christ is the Lord of my life from this day. I have eternal life through Him, and I'm born again in His Name. Thank you, Lord, for saving my soul! I'm now a child of God. Amen.

Congratulations! You are now a child of God.

About the Ministry

Felix Harcourt Ministries is established with a vision to unveil the true nature of God to the nations and people of the world; to demonstrate the character of the Spirit, with the mission of "Connecting people to Jesus, Changing Lives."

Our Hope for this Book

We aim to get this book to every sick child in the hospital or at home.